ADULT PIANO Adventures®
Popular

Timeless Hits
and Popular
Favorites

2

Arranged by Nancy and Randall Faber

Production Coordinator: Jon Ophoff
Editor: Isabel Otero Bowen
Cover: Terpstra Design, San Francisco
Engraving: Dovetree Productions, Inc.

FABER
PIANO ADVENTURES®

ISBN 978-1-61677-190-4

FOREWORD

When someone mentions the song *Make You Feel My Love*, do you picture Bob Dylan or Adele? Do you recall Gloria Gaynor's soulful *I Will Survive* or the bass-driven cover by Cake? When you think of *The Sound of Silence*, are you reminded of Paul Simon's haunting original or the powerful new performance by Disturbed? Do you carry a torch for Elton John's *Your Song* or Ewan McGregor's remarkable interpretation in the film *Moulin Rouge?* It is a testament to the staying power of these and other evergreen hits that the stars of today are drawn to make their own renditions.

Indeed, the appeal of popular music spans generations and genres. Enjoy folk tunes like *Ashokan Farewell* and *Bridge Over Troubled Water*, movie themes from James Bond and Batman, Broadway numbers from *Evita* and *A Little Night Music*, and chart-toppers performed by Michael Jackson, Billy Joel, the Beatles, and more.

Adult Piano Adventures® Popular Book 2 provides this variety, yet with accessible arrangements for the progressing pianist. These timeless hits are presented in approximate order of difficulty. You may advance through the book alongside method studies, or jump to all your favorites. Refer to the optional chord symbols above the staff to guide your understanding and personal expression.

Whether you prefer to *"Let It Go"* with Disney or take it *"Smooth"* with Santana, let creating music at the piano become part of you.

TABLE OF CONTENTS

Over the Rainbow

from *The Wizard of Oz*

Music by Harold Arlen
Lyric by E. Y. "Yip" Harburg

5

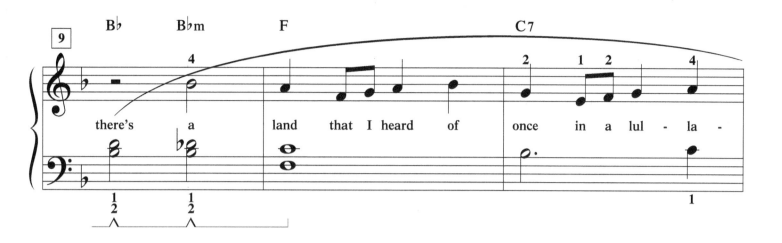

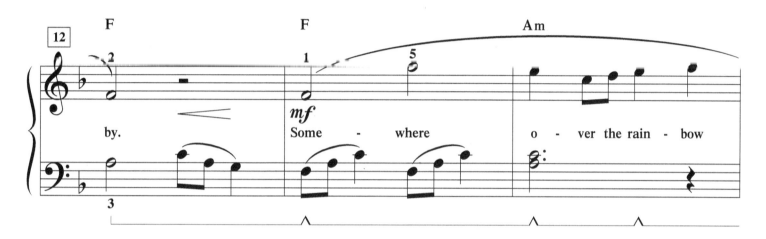

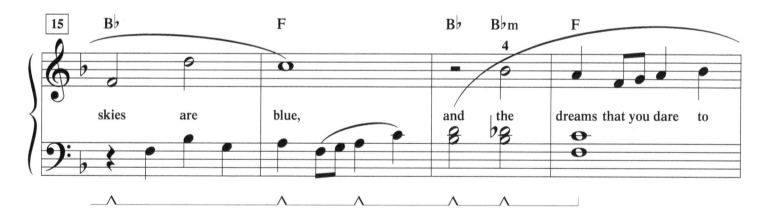

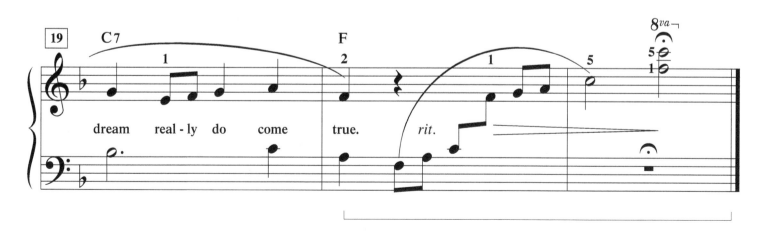

FF3033

Ain't No Mountain High Enough

Words and Music by
Nickolas Ashford and Valerie Simpson

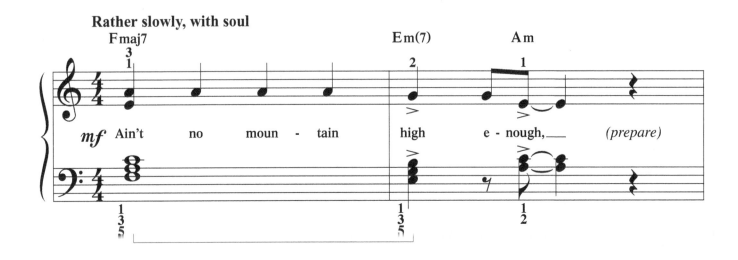

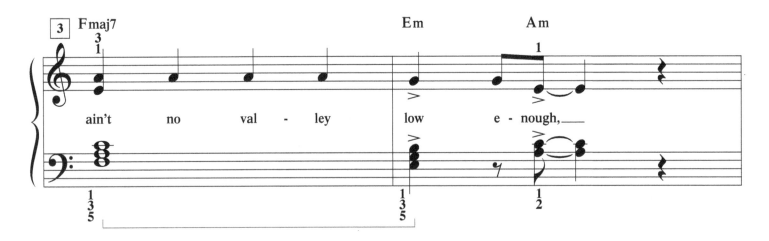

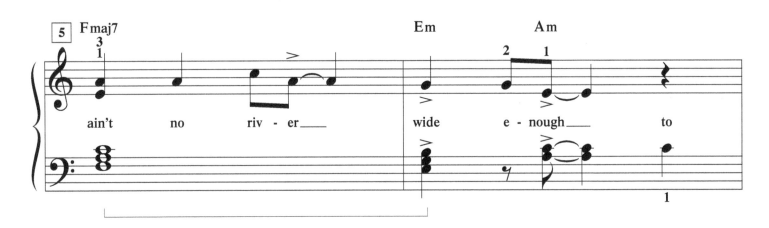

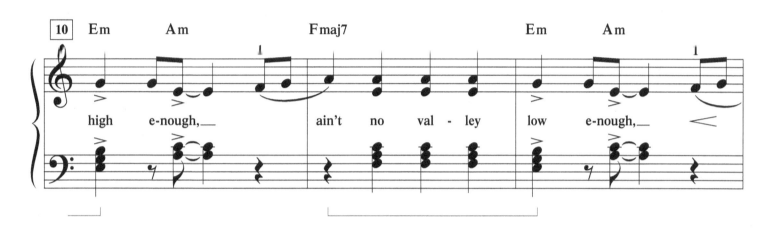

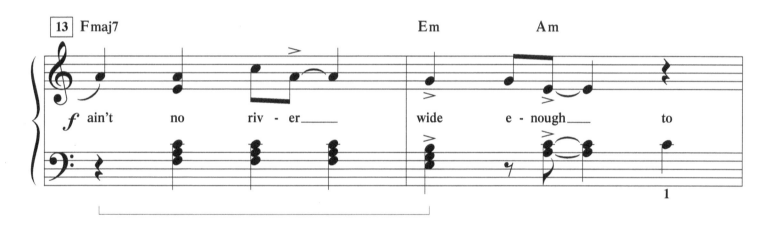

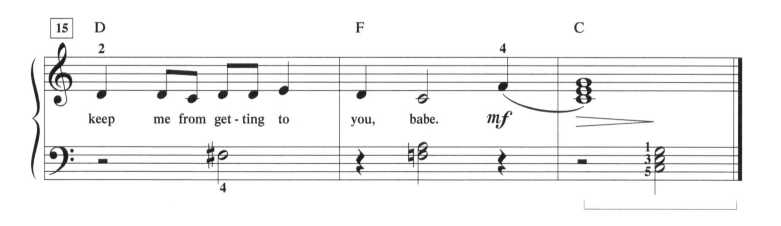

Don't Cry for Me Argentina

from *Evita*

Words by Tim Rice
Music by Andrew Lloyd Webber

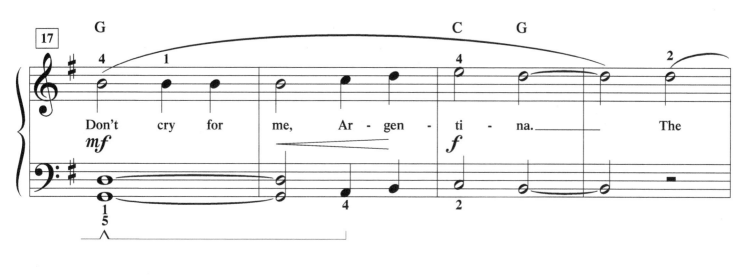

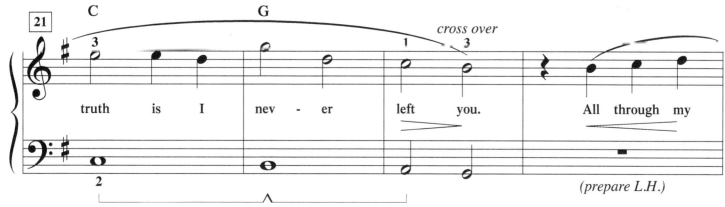

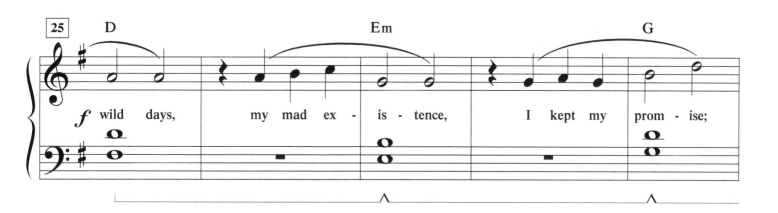

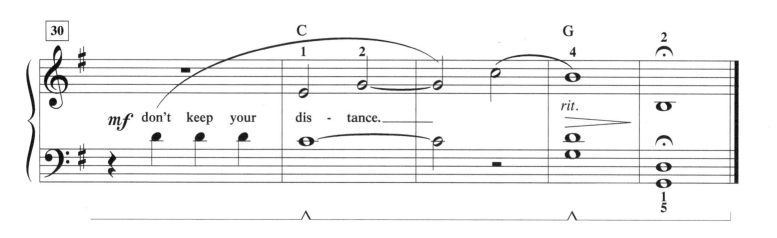

FF3033

Ashokan Farewell
Theme from the PBS series *The Civil War*

By Jay Ungar

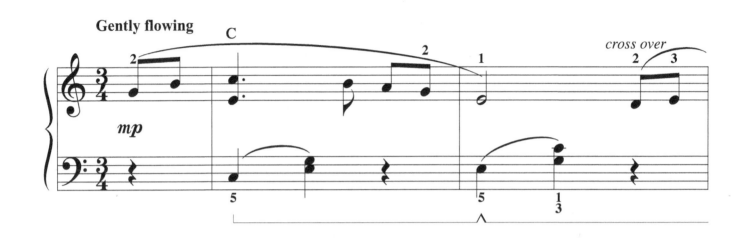

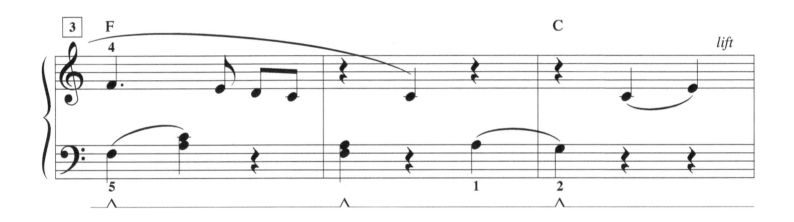

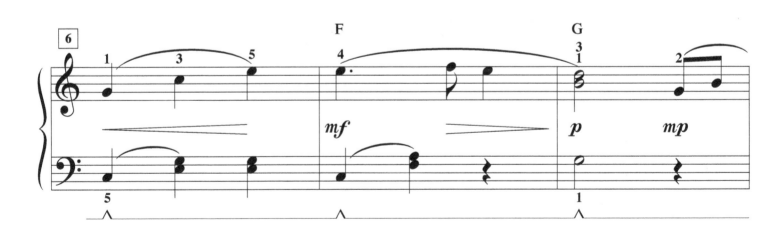

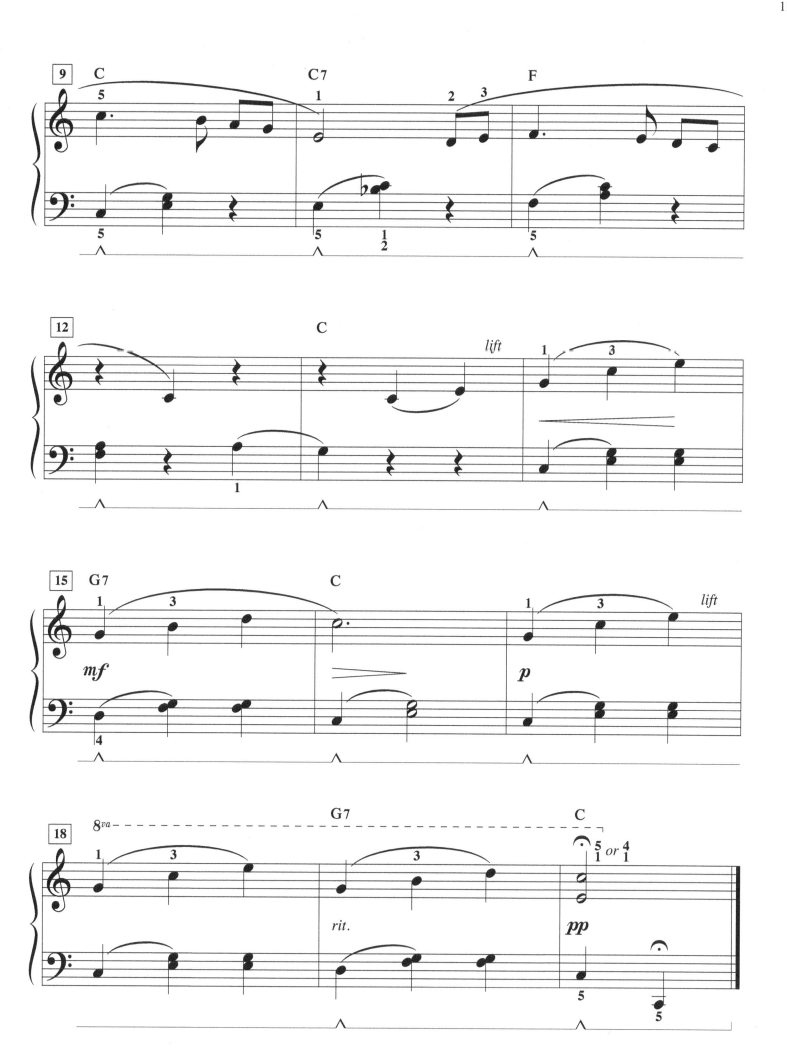

Let It Go
from *Frozen*

Music and Lyrics by
Kristen Anderson-Lopez and Robert Lopez

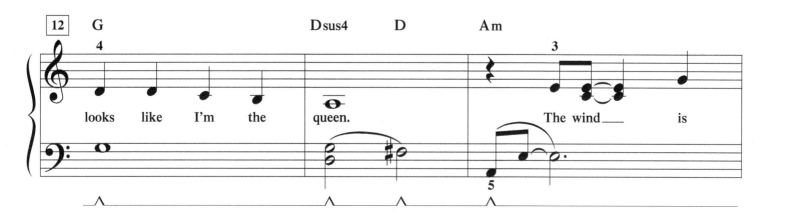

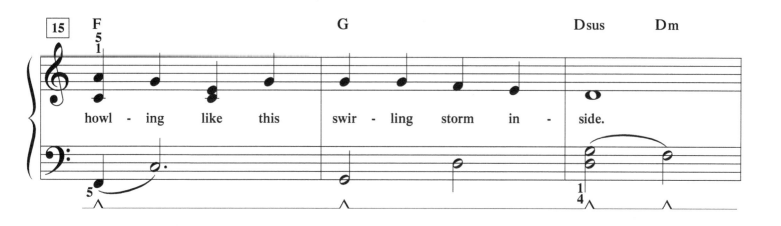

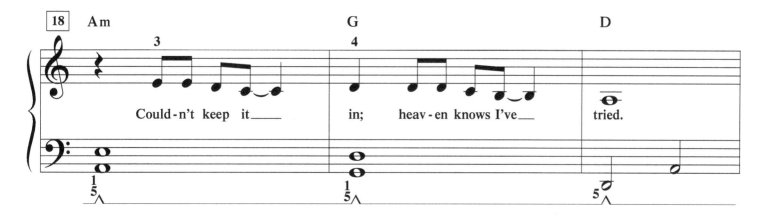

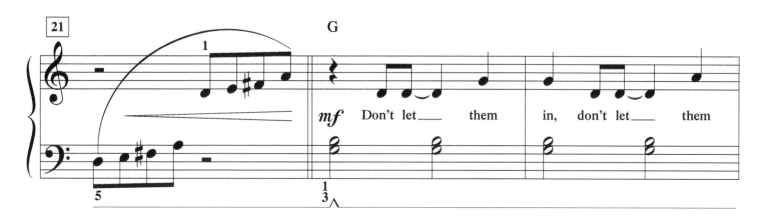

14

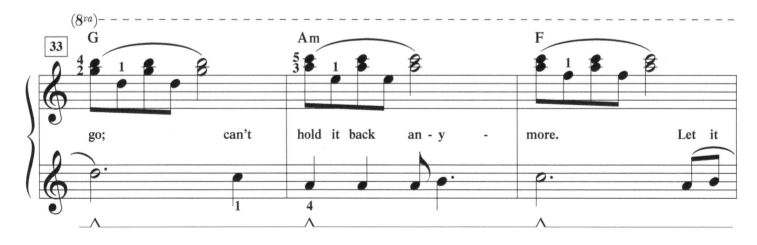

Somewhere, My Love

Lara's Theme from *Doctor Zhivago*

Lyric by Paul Francis Webster
Music by Maurice Jarre

Singin' in the Rain

Lyric by Arthur Freed
Music by Nacio Herb Brown

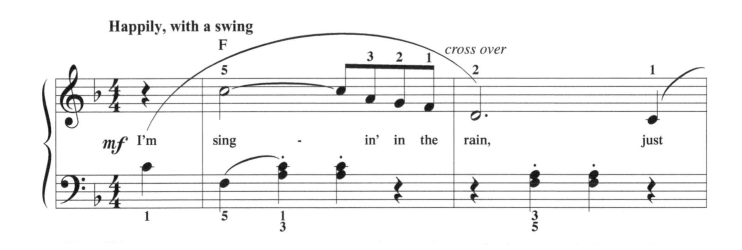

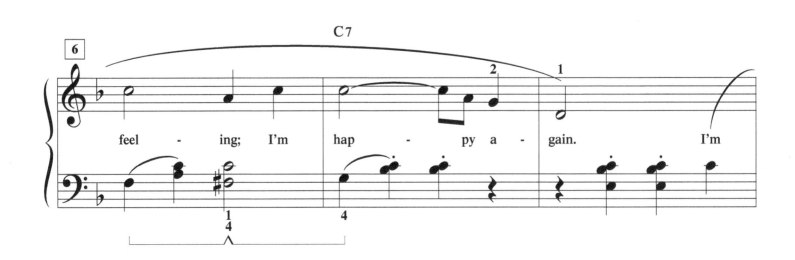

Batman Theme

Words and Music by
Neal Hefti

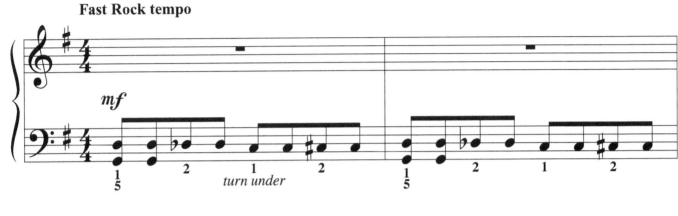

22

Bridge Over Troubled Water

Words and Music by
Paul Simon

23

FF3033

All I Have to Do Is Dream

Words and Music by
Boudleaux Bryant

I Will Survive

Words and Music by
Dino Fekaris and Frederick J. Perren

28

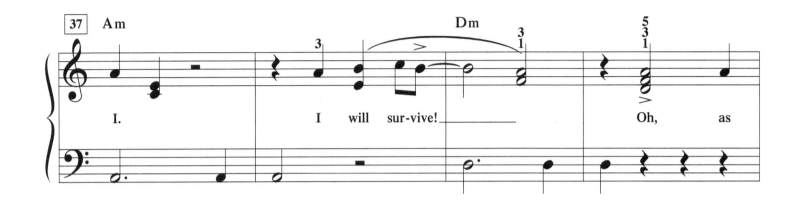

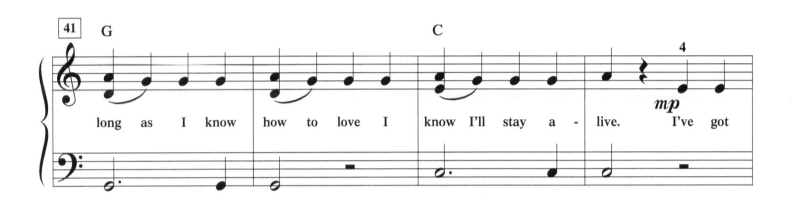

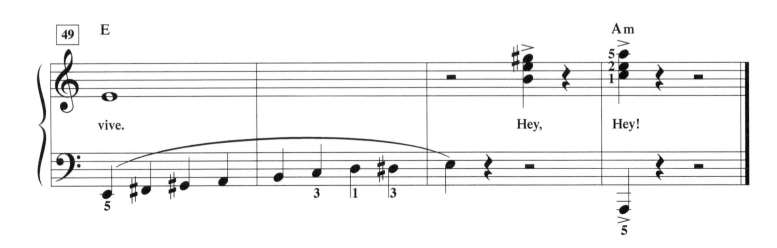

Your Song

**Words and Music by
Elton John and Bernie Taupin**

FF3033

30
Gm7
B♭
Dm
now that it's done, I hope you don't mind, I
33
Dm/C
Dm/B
B♭
hope you don't mind, that I put down in words how
36
F/A
B♭
B♭
won - der - ful life is while you're in the
39
C
F
B♭/F
world.
mp
43
C/F
B♭/F
F
p

The James Bond Theme

By Monty Norman

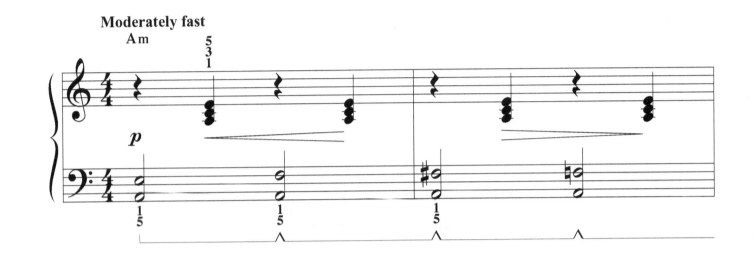

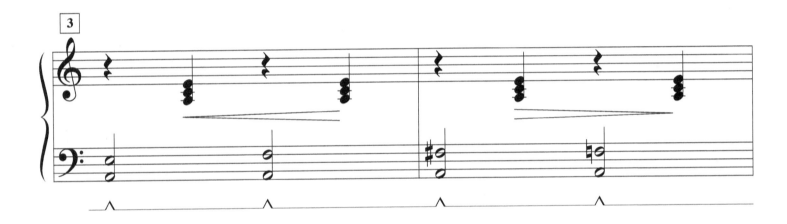

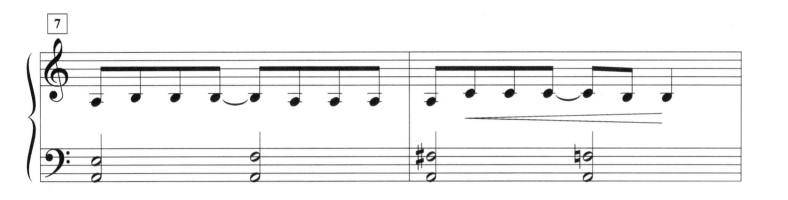

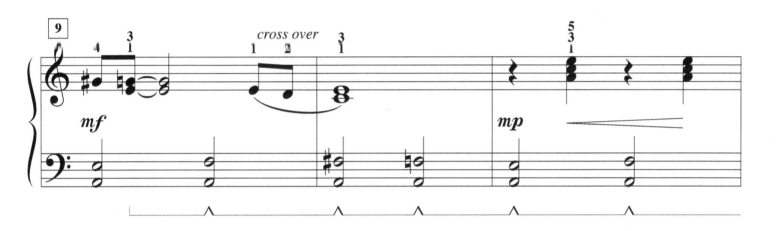

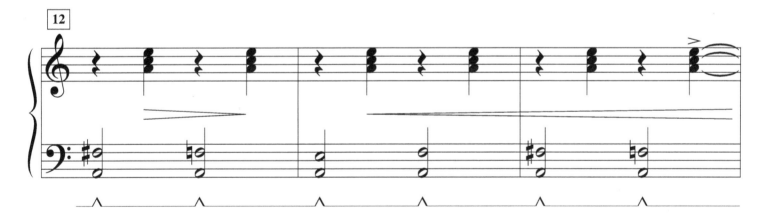

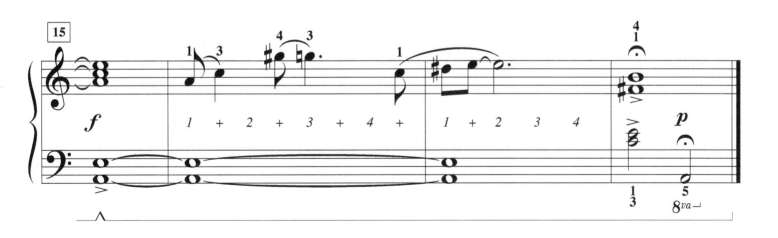

Hey Jude

Words and Music by
John Lennon and Paul McCartney

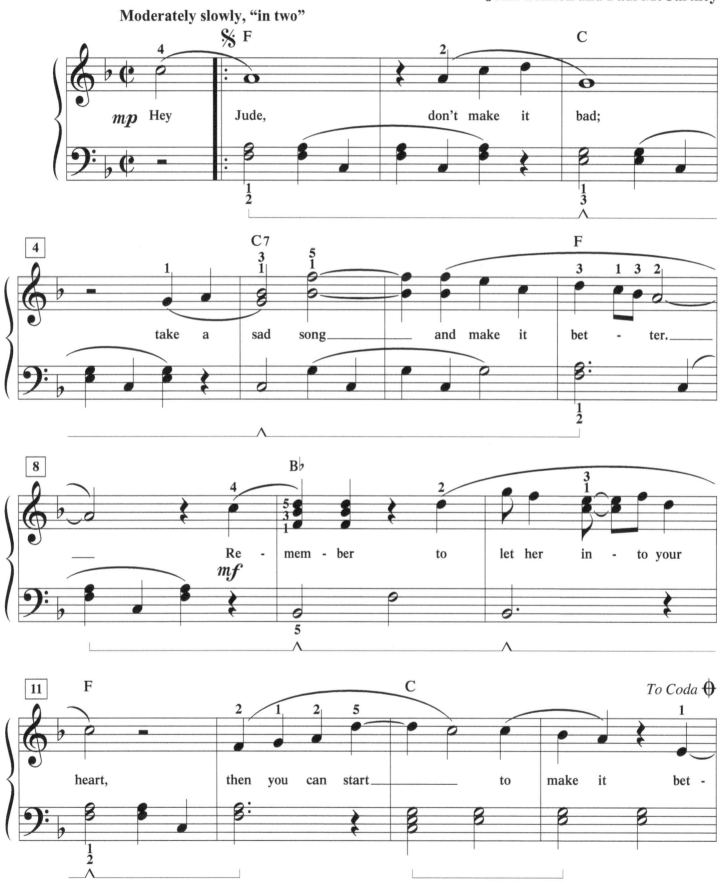

FF3033

36

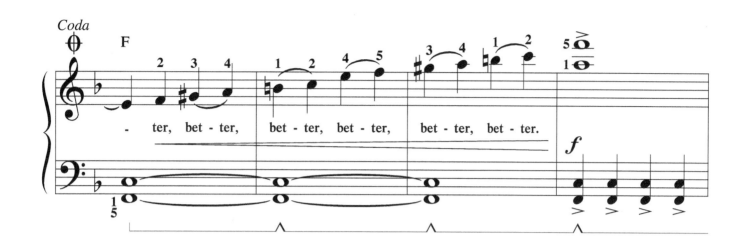

FF3033

Sweet Caroline

Words and Music by
Neil Diamond

Make You Feel My Love

Words and Music by
Bob Dylan

A Whole New World
from Walt Disney's *Aladdin*

Music by Alan Menken
Lyrics by Tim Rice

I can show____ you the world, shin - ing, shim - mer - ing splen - did.
I can o - pen your eyes, take you won - der by won - der

Tell me prin - cess, now when did you last
o - ver, side - ways and un - der on a

FF3033

44

Stand by Me

**Words and Music by Jerry Leiber,
Mike Stoller, and Ben E. King**

48

I Will Always Love You

Words and Music by
Dolly Parton

Additional Lyrics

2. Bittersweet memories
   That is all I'm taking with me.
   So, goodbye, please don't cry.
   We both know I'm not what you need. *To Chorus*

3. I hope life treats you kind
   And I hope you have all you've dreamed of.
   I wish you joy and happiness.
   But above all this, I wish you love. *To Chorus*

Thriller

from Michael Jackson's album *Thriller*

Words and Music by
Rod Temperton

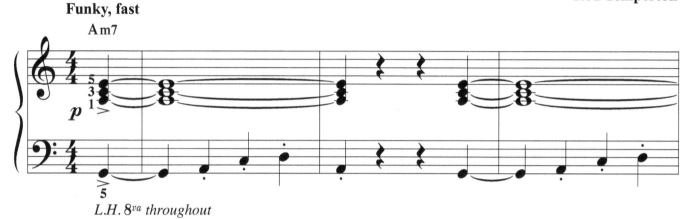

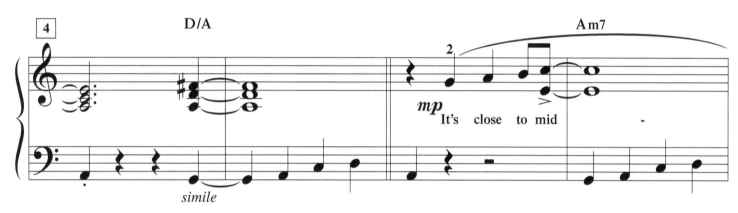

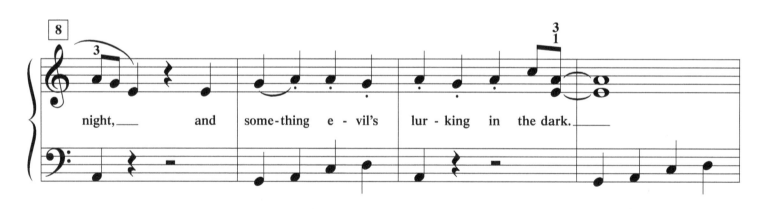

54

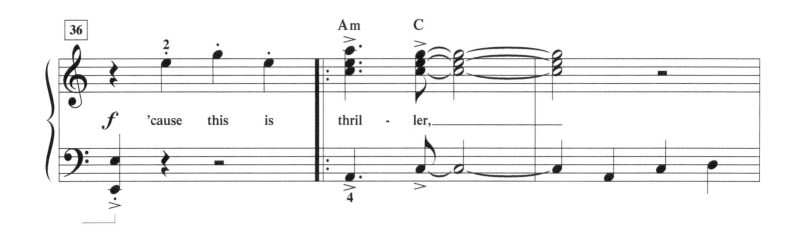

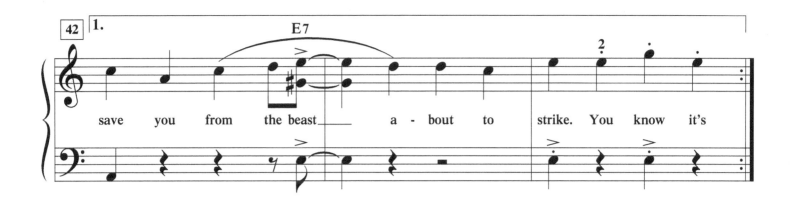

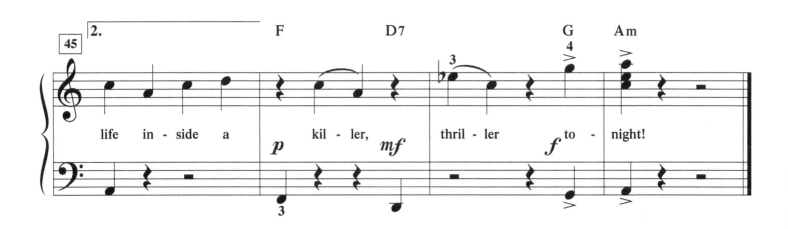

Rolling in the Deep

**Words and Music by
Adele Adkins and Paul Epworth**

FF3033

56

57

FF3033

Send in the Clowns

from the musical *A Little Night Music*

**Words and Music by
Stephen Sondheim**

Smooth

Words by Rob Thomas
Music by Rob Thomas and Itaal Shur

62

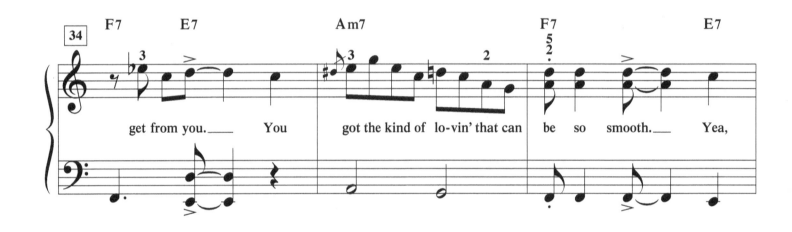

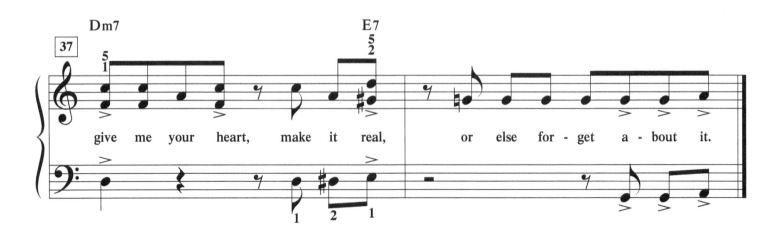

You Raise Me Up

Words and Music by
Brendan Graham and Rolf Lovland

FF3033

64

The Sound of Silence

Words and Music by
Paul Simon

68

FF3033

Piano Man

Words and Music by
Billy Joel

72

FF3033

Additional Lyrics

3. Now Paul is a real estate novelist,
   who never had time for a wife,
   and he's talkin' with Davy, who's still in the Navy
   and probably will be for life.
   And the waitress is practicing politics
   as the businessmen slowly get stoned.
   Yes, they're sharing a drink they call loneliness,
   but it's better than drinkin' alone.

4. It's a pretty good crowd for a Saturday,
   and the manager gives me a smile
   'cause he knows that it's me they've been comin' to see
   to forget about life for awhile.
   And the piano sounds like a carnival,
   and the microphone smells like a beer,
   and they sit at the bar and put bread in my jar
   and say, "Man, what are you doin' here?"

When a Man Loves a Woman

Words and Music by
Calvin Lewis and Andrew Wright

FF3033

DICTIONARY OF MUSICAL TERMS

DYNAMIC MARKS

$\boldsymbol{pp}$	$\boldsymbol{p}$	$\boldsymbol{mp}$	$\boldsymbol{mf}$	$\boldsymbol{f}$	$\boldsymbol{ff}$
pianissimo very soft	*piano* soft	*mezzo piano* moderately soft	*mezzo forte* moderately loud	*forte* loud	*fortissimo* very loud

crescendo (cresc.)
Play gradually louder.

diminuendo (dim.) or decrescendo (decresc.)
Play gradually softer.

SIGN	TERM	DEFINITION
	a tempo	Return to the original tempo (speed).
	accent mark	Play this note louder.
	accidental	Sharps, flats, or naturals added to a piece and not in the key signature.
Gadd6	**added tone chord**	A chord consisting of a triad plus an added note an interval above the chord's root (Ex. Gadd6, played G-B-D-E).
	chord	Three or more tones sounding together.
C/F	**chord/bass note**	The first letter is the chord name. The second is the bass note.
	chord symbol	The letter name of a chord (shown above the staff) indicating the harmony. A lowercase "m" is used to show minor.
	chord inversion	Rearranging the notes of a chord. Ex. C-E-G may invert to E-G-C or G-C-E.
	coda	Ending section.
¢	**common time**	4/4 time.
¢	**cut time (alla breve)**	2/2 time. The half note receives the beat (two half-note beats per measure).
D.C. al Coda	**Da Capo al Coda**	Return to the beginning and play to ⊕, then jump to the *Coda* (ending).
D.S. al Coda	**Dal Segno al Coda**	Return to the 𝄋 sign and play to ⊕, then jump to the *Coda* (ending).
	damper pedal	The right pedal, which sustains the sound, played with the right foot.
	dotted quarter note	A dot adds half the value to the note. A dotted quarter is the equivalent of a quarter note tied to an eighth note.
	eighth rest	Silence for the value of an eighth note.
	fermata	Hold this note longer than its normal value.
1. 2.	**1st and 2nd endings**	Play the 1st ending and repeat from the beginning. Then play the 2nd ending, skipping over the 1st ending.
♭	**flat**	A flat lowers a note one half step.
	half step	The distance from one key to the very closest key on the keyboard. (Ex. C-C♯, or E-F)
	interval	The distance between two musical tones, keys on the keyboard, or notes on the staff. (Ex. 2nd, 3rd, 4th, 5th)
	key signature	The key signature appears at the beginning of each line of music. It indicates sharps or flats to be used throughout the piece.

	ledger line	A short line used to extend the staff.
	legato	Smooth, connected.
	natural	A natural (always a white key) cancels a sharp or a flat.
N.C.	**no chord**	Chord symbol that indicates no chord being played, or implied harmony.
	octave	The interval which spans 8 letter names. (Ex. C to C)
8va	*ottava*	Play one octave higher (or lower) than written.
	pedal change	Shows the up-down motion of the damper pedal.
	phrase	A musical sentence. A phrase is often shown by a slur, also called a phrase mark.
	poco a poco	Little by little.
	repeat sign	Play the music within the repeat signs again.
rit.	*ritardando*	Gradually slowing down.
	root	The chord tone that is the letter name of the chord.
	root position	The letter name of the chord is the lowest note.
	scale	From the Latin word *scala*, meaning "ladder." The notes of a scale move up or down by 2nds (steps).
G7	**7th chord**	A chord consisting of a triad plus a note forming an interval of a 7th above the chord's root. Can be a minor 7th (Ex. G7, played G-B-D-F) or a major 7th (Gmaj7, played G-B-D-F♯).
♯	**sharp**	A sharp raises a note one half step.
	simile	Similarly.
	sixteenth notes	Four sixteenth notes equal one quarter note.
	slur	A curved line that indicates legato playing.
	staccato	Detached, disconnected.
sus or **sus4**	**suspended-4 chord**	A three-note chord that uses the 4th instead of the 3rd.
	swing rhythm	Eighth notes played in a long-short pattern.
	tempo	The speed of the music.
	tie	A curved line that connects two notes on the same line or space. Hold for the total counts of both notes.
	time signature	Two numbers at the beginning of a piece (one above the other). The top number indicates the number of beats per measure; the bottom number represents the note receiving the beat.
	triad	A 3-note chord built in 3rds.
	triplet	Three eighth notes to a quarter note.
	upbeat (pick-up note)	The note(s) of an incomplete opening measure.
	whole step	The distance of two half steps.

FF3033

ALPHABETICAL INDEX OF TITLES